THE STORY OF

Portraits

40,000 years of the human face

by Mick Manning and Brita Granström

W

FRANKLIN WATTS

LONDON•SYDNEY

Contents

Our Story Begins ...

A portrait is a word we use to describe a work of art that represents a real person or sometimes an imaginary one. Portraits can be self-portraits, power-portraits, religious icons, propaganda portraits, publicity shots or even mugshots and they can be lots of other things too. In this book we've chosen lots of exciting examples of portraits from many countries and cultures; some are well-known but others you may never have seen before.

So, get ready to meet people, both real and imaginary.
We must begin thousands of years ago ...

I'm going to carve this tusk into a face.

Venus of Brassempouy
France, about 23,000 BCE

Imagine exploring a prehistoric cave and coming face to face with this tiny head. This small fragment of a larger sculpture was carved from mammoth ivory one cold day, during the last Ice Age about 25,000 years ago.

Who was she?
It's so long ago no-one knows for sure. A long-forgotten goddess or a real person – what do you think?

The Lady of the Well   Iraq, 800 BCE

This beautiful 16-cm-high carving represents the goddess Ishtar. She was discovered by the archaeologist Max Mallowan at the bottom of a well in what was once the Assyrian city of Nimrod in Iraq.

Who was she?
Ishtar, also known as 'Queen of the Universe', was a powerful goddess worshipped in Middle-Eastern countries long ago.

Two Girls at Play Ancient Greece, 400 BCE

The accuracy and beauty of the large ancient Greek sculptures of heroes, warriors, gods and goddesses set standards for future artists who called the style 'Classical'. But there were also exquisite smaller works such as this 13-cm-high terracotta sculpture, a small snapshot from the everyday life of two young ancient Greek women quietly playing knucklebones together.

Who were they?
Their identities are lost, but they seem to be well-dressed, with leisure time to play games. Like all ancient Greek sculptures, this would once have been realistically painted and traces of paint can still be seen on the little figurines.

Terracotta Army
China, 246–208 BCE

This army of 8,000 life-size terracotta warriors once protected the tomb of the Chinese emperor Qin Shi Huang. There are only 10 basic 'factory-made' face shapes but, by adding clay details such as moustaches and eyebrows, the artists have made each of the 8,000 faces unique.

Terentius Neo and his Wife Ancient Rome, 55–79 CE

This beautiful fresco from the lost city of Pompeii was buried under a deep layer of ash after the volcano Mount Vesuvius erupted in 79 CE.

Who were they?
Evidence suggests this couple probably had a local bakery business.

Look, it's us!

Religious Portraits

As we have already seen with Ishtar (page 4), artists of different faiths have been inspired to make iconic religious portraits as a way of putting a face to a name and to have a figure to worship in front of. The Islamic faith does not do this, as illustrating their religious figures is seen as disrespectful.

Lakshmi on a Lotus

by Ravi Varma.
Painting. India. 1898

There are many wonderful images of Hindu deities. This is Lakshmi beautifully imagined by Ravi Varma. Lakshmi was the goddess of wealth, business and fortune and she was born out of an ocean of milk.

Tongil Daebul

Buddha, artist unknown, Sculpture, South Korea, 1993

He looks so peaceful.

Tongil Daebul is a huge modern Buddha made of gilt bronze. He is 14.6 metres tall. As he sits on a lotus pedestal with his eyes closed in meditation, his hands are in the 'Mundra' position – a symbol of enlightenment and peace.

Madonna and Child

artist unknown, Mosaic, Sinai, Egypt, 13th Century

This ancient Byzantine icon with the Virgin Mary's hand introducing Jesus is called a *Hodegetria* and is one of the earliest types of Christian portraits. The Christian church became a great sponsor of artists, especially during the Middle Ages.

Let's turn the page and look at some portraits in more detail, starting with what is perhaps the most famous ancient face of all …

Tutankhamun

by an unknown artist

This golden mask once covered the mummified body of Tutankhamun, an Egyptian pharaoh. Pharaohs believed they were gods and this artist has made sure this portrait of Tutankhamun is both recognisable as the teenage king and as Osiris, god of the afterlife. The incredible detail shows the ruler's striped pharaoh's head-cloth crowned by the royal insignia of a cobra and a vulture. Like many other pharaohs, Tutankhamun was buried in a secret underground tomb in an area of desert land known as the Valley of the Kings. This mask is now on display in the Egyptian Museum in Cairo.

Tutankhamun will be remembered as a god.

Who was he?
Tutankhamun, also known as the boy king, ruled during the 18th Dynasty between 1332 to 1323 BCE. This beautiful mask was made by a skilled artist from pressed and beaten copper and gold, inlaid with coloured glass and precious gemstones.

The mask was discovered when the archaeologist Howard Carter opened Tutankhamun's tomb in 1925.

Kublai Khan

by Araniko, 1245–1306

The artist of this painting was a man named Araniko who worked in the court of the fearsome ruler Kublai Khan (1215-1294). This famous portrait of Kublai Khan was painted just after his death and skilfully commemorates the ruthless leader as he wanted to be remembered: looking thirty years younger and in his prime. Araniko gives him a wise expression; notice the laughter lines around his eyes and his neatly combed beard and eyebrows. Under his hat we can just see the bristles of his shaved head. Araniko painted this portrait with coloured inks on silk.

Who was he?
Kublai Khan succeeded his grandfather Genghis and began the Yuan dynasty ruling present-day China, Mongolia, Korea and parts of Siberia. He was a strong leader but also a philosopher who encouraged the arts.

I will paint Kublai Khan as a wise man, not as a killer.

The artist, Araniko, was also a skilled architect. His best known building is the White Stupa of Miaoying Temple, once the largest building of its day. It still stands in modern-day Beijing, China.

Portrait of a Woman with a Man at a Casement

by Fra Filippo Lippi, c. 1406–1469

This painting, created by Fra Filippo Lippi in c. 1440, is considered to be one of the first portraits to show someone inside a home. It was painted in Italy at the beginning of an age of new ideas in the arts and sciences we call 'the Renaissance'. Notice the lady's sumptuous clothes and her sleeve with the embroidered word 'Lealtà' which means 'faithful'. This is a clue that the portrait may have been a betrothal portrait – a painting on the theme of marriage. Look at the man's loving gaze. Is he proposing or perhaps making vows of loyalty to her?
What do you think?

Fra Filippo Lippi

Who were they?
No one knows for sure but the man's coat of arms is of the well-to-do Scolari, a rich and powerful family from Florence, Italy.

As a young man Fra Filippo Lippi was captured by pirates. He earned his freedom by drawing their portraits.

Look at the work of other Renaissance masters such as Sandro Botticelli who was trained by Fra Filippo Lippi.

Portrait of a Girl

by Petrus Christus. c. 1410–1475

Compare this portrait by Dutch artist Petrus Christus, from c. 1468, to the Fra Filippo Lippi painting on the previous page. Notice the difference – this girl is looking us in the eye and that makes it one of the most groundbreaking paintings in art history. Her hair is fashionably drawn back under her conical hat, and the fabric elegantly frames her jawline. Christus employs the recently developed Renaissance technique of *chiaroscuro* (a dramatic use of light and dark) to light up her face against the shadowy background wall. Best of all, he has noticed and painted her slightly uneven eyes. With her thoughtful, although rather bored, expression Christus brings this medieval teenager to life. What do you think she is thinking as she stares back at us across the centuries?

Who was she?
It is thought that the sitter is Lady Ann or possibly Lady Margaret Talbot, one of the daughters of Lord John Talbot who visited Bruges in 1468 for a royal wedding.

Self-portrait at the Age of 13

by Albrecht Dürer, 1471–1528

On the previous page we met a medieval girl so now let's meet a medieval boy. This skillful self-portrait by the German artist Albrecht Dürer is a line drawing made when he was only 13 years old. It's one of the earliest known European self-portraits and was made when Dürer was studying in his father's goldsmith workshop. He was clearly proud of this drawing because much later he wrote on it: "This I drew myself from a mirror in the year 1484, when I was still a child."

Who was he?
Albrecht Dürer already had a great reputation as a painter by his mid-twenties. He spent time studying in Italy where he met the artist Raphael, and introduced Renaissance painting to Northern Europe.

Look at some of the portrait paintings of the artist Raphael and see if you can spot any influences.

People will look at my drawing one day and ask, "What is he pointing at?"

17

The Mona Lisa

by Leonardo da Vinci, 1452–1519

With her gentle smile, Leonardo da Vinci's world-famous painting, the *Mona Lisa*, really does seem to be alive. To achieve that feeling of direct eye contact Leonardo has placed the horizon line on a level with her eyes. He also uses a paint blending technique called *sfumato* meaning 'smokey' to create a soft-focus effect.

Da Vinci worked on the painting between 1503–1519. Recently, using new scanning technology, scientists discovered he had originally painted Lisa wearing hairpins and even a pearl headdress before he decided 'less is more' and overpainted them to create this masterpiece.

> Relax. My soft-focus sfumato technique will make you look ten years younger my lady!

Who was she?
The name 'Mona Lisa', properly spelled in Italian as Monna Lisa, translates into English as 'My Lady Lisa' or 'Madam Lisa'. She was possibly Lisa del Giocondo, a member of a well-to-do Tuscan family and the wife of a wealthy silk merchant.

Portrait of an African Man (Christophle le More)

by Jan Mostaert, c. 1475–1553

This portrait is by the Dutch artist Jan Mostaert. It dates from about 1525 and it's one of the earliest European portraits of a man of African descent. Although we can't be entirely sure who he is, we can see that he is well-dressed. With his hand on his sword pommel and his expensive-looking clothes he is clearly a professional. Notice the artist's clever use of green, the complimentary colour to red and how Mostaert's shadowy green background 'pushes' the man's red velvet shirt and cap forward and really brings him to life.

Who was he?
Experts at Amsterdam's Rijksmuseum (who own the painting) suggest that the pilgrim's badge in his cap is a clue that he may have been Christophle le More, a man known to have worked for Charles V, the Holy Roman Emperor.

Make sure you paint my lovely gloves!

Can you find these objects in the painting?

A pilgrim's badge. *This shows 'Our Lady of Halle' and is likely a souvenir of his visit to the statue of the Virgin Mary in Halle, Belgium.*

Jewels. *These precious stones can be found on the beautifully decorated bag hanging from his belt.*

Kid gloves. *Look at his expensive, tight leather goatskin gloves.*

Portrait of Antonietta Gonsalvus

by Lavinia Fontana, 1552–1614

This portrait, painted in 1583 by Lavinia Fontana, shows Antonietta Gonsalvus (or Gonzalez), a ten-year-old girl with a rare illness then called 'werewolf syndrome'. Lavinia presents young Antonietta with great respect and shows us not a circus freak but a well-dressed little girl who looks us in the eye with intelligence and a smile. Lavinia was taught to paint by her father, a master at the famous Bologna School of Painting in Italy. Her portrait skills were in such demand that when she married she continued to earn her living as a painter despite having eleven children. Her husband took care of the children and also acted as her agent.

Who was she?
Antonietta was the daughter of Pedro Gonsalvus, the first known sufferer of werewolf syndrome. Although well treated at court, the family was viewed by many as entertaining objects of curiosity. In her hand she is holding a paper giving the history of her family.

Don Francisco de Arobe and Sons Pedro and Domingo

by Andrés Sánchez Galque,
c. 1590–1661

This group portrait, from 1599, shows us Francisco de Arobe, the governor of a town on the South American coast of Ecuador. Together with his sons, Pedro and Domingo, he swore allegiance to the King of Spain in return for political power.

This painting was made as a gift for the king by the artist Andrés Sánchez Galque, an indigenous man from Ecuador, educated as a painter by Catholic friars. Notice how Andrés skilfully paints the fabulous costumes, their gold and shell jewellery, not to mention their formidable spears. This is a power-portrait intended to portray Francisco and his sons as strong allies to the colonial power of Spain but with their hats politely doffed in respect to their king.

DON FRAN. DEAROBE. 5 6 .Ã^{os}

DÕDOMÍNGO. 1 8 .Ã^s

PHILÍPPO. 3. CATHOLICO
REGÍ. HÍSPANIARq
ÍNDÍARq Q3DNO. SVO
DOCTOR. IOANES. DEL. BARRÍO
A SEPVLVEDA. AVDÍ TOR. SVE
CANCELLARÍÆ. DEL. QVÍTO
SVÍS EXPEN SÍS. FÍE RÍ.
CVRAVÍT
ANNO. 1599

AR. SĤS. GAÕ.
:ñt. de 9̃. f.

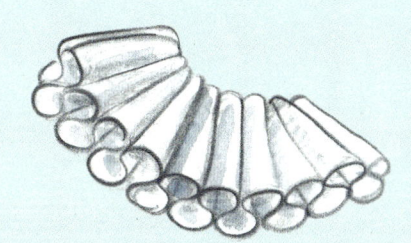

Who were they?

Francisco was the son of an escaped enslaved
African man. His sons, Pedro and Domingo, were
his henchmen. They all wear a mixture of South
American and Spanish fashions: gold jewellery in
their ears and noses, and Spanish neck ruffs.

Girl with a Pearl Earring

by Johannes Vermeer, 1632–1675

This captivating portrait was painted by Johannes Vermeer in around 1665 during the 'Golden Age' of Dutch painting. Vermeer has used the technique of *chiaroscuro* (see page 15) to light up his model's face. Look at that large earring. It was originally considered to be a huge pearl but may actually be a Venetian glass bauble and on a very small ear. This is an example of a 'tronie' – a portrait using an artist's model dressed theatrically to symbolise, for example, beauty, old age or a biblical figure. She seems to be wearing what was then known as a Turkish head scarf, but it's unlikely we will ever know for sure who this beautiful portrait is meant to represent. What do you think?

Who was she?
One theory suggests the model may have been Vermeer's own daughter Maria, who was about 12 at that time. Is that why the earring looks so big?

I love this Turkish headscarf father!

Those earrings look huge on your tiny ears Maria.

Self-portrait at the Age of 63

by Rembrandt van Rijn, 1606–1669

After a long career as a painter, Dutch artist Rembrandt painted this self-portrait in old age. As he looks at us, his soulful eyes seem desperate to tell us about his life; perhaps jolly tales about his early success or sad stories about the hardships he has seen. Rembrandt has used not only *chiaroscuro* (see page 15) to create depth but *impasto* (layers of thick oil paint) to show his ageing skin. Sixty-three was considered very old in those days and in this honest portrait of old age, painted only months before he died, Rembrandt shows us a tired man who has lived life to the full and experienced both riches and poverty.

Who was he?
Rembrandt painted many self-portraits throughout his life and they are often named as his greatest creative triumphs. After early success with etchings and large scale works such as The Night Watch, *Rembrandt fell into poverty.*

There are so many stories I could tell you ...

Mr and Mrs Andrews

by Thomas Gainsborough, 1727–1788

This Romantic double-portrait by Thomas Gainsborough was painted in Suffolk, England, when he was only 23. It combines Gainsborough's two favourite genres, portraiture and landscape. It shows the recently married couple, Robert and Frances Andrews, posing with their dog and gun, proudly showing us their 3,000-acre country estate. They look out at us with a smug expression that seems to say 'We own all this

land, as far as the eye can see!' Gainsborough has put in so much detail that our eyes can explore the late-summer countryside: look at the sky, it promises rain or even thunder. Can you spot the sheep, already lying down in a far away field? Can you see the wheat harvested into stooks and the church spire among the branches?

Thomas Gainsborough

Who were they?
The Andrews were wealthy landowners who lived in rural Suffolk, England.

Opinions vary as to what the patch of bare canvas on Mrs Andrews' lap was reserved for. Some see a rough sketch of a dead pheasant with tail and wings outstretched; others think it was a space left for their baby daughter.

I am not having that dirty pheasant on this clean dress, Robert!'

Napoleon Crossing the Alps

by Jacques-Louis David, 1748-1825

Jacques-Louis David was considered the greatest French painter of his generation and a French Revolutionary. This iconic portrait of his hero Napoleon, completed in 1801, is an example of the Neoclassical, a theatrical style influenced by Classical art and the Renaissance. David idolised his emperor and portrays him full of bravado and daring spirit, leading his troops across the Alps. His composition makes us look up at him to add importance. Just look at the 'cinematic' drama of the dark, rolling clouds and Napoleon's red cloak flapping in the wind as he points the way to victory. As if carved into the rocks, David has painted the names of Hannibal and Charlemagne (Karolus Magnus), two famous heroes from ancient times who both led their armies across the Alps.

Who was he?
Napoleon Bonaparte (1769–1821) conquered large parts of Europe until his mighty army was finally defeated in 1815. Many of his ideas have influenced modern-day politics, yet the Napoleonic Wars killed millions of people.

My legs are getting tired Dad. Can I take a break now?

Bonaparte was too busy to pose for the portrait. David used a sculpture as reference for Napoleon's face and made his own son dress up in one of Napoleon's old uniforms and pose on a ladder.

Self-portrait

by Sarah Biffin, 1784–1850

This undated self-portrait by English artist Sarah Biffin is extraordinary because Biffin was born without arms or legs. Incredibly, she taught herself to write, draw and paint by using her mouth and teeth to grip pens and brushes. Sadly, she began her artistic life as a travelling fairground attraction and things may have remained so if Earl George Douglas, a wealthy aristocrat, hadn't talent-spotted her and taken her to London. Douglas took Sarah under his wing and paid for her to have watercolour lessons. She opened her own studio in London, painting portrait miniatures for wealthy clients. In a time long before photography was ever invented, portrait miniature paintings were the snapshots of their day. Sarah exhibited at the Royal Academy and was even awarded a pension by Queen Victoria.

Who was she?

At 13 Sarah was apprenticed to a travelling showman and 'exhibited' at country fairs painting fair-goers' portraits.

Then, one day, Earl George Douglas walked into her life …

I'm going to take you away from this place Miss Biffin!

He helped her set up her own fashionable studio in London and she became famous..

In Sarah Biffin's lifetime it was fashionable to own a miniature portrait painting of yourself or a loved one.

Portrait miniatures are tiny artworks painted with exquisite detail. Look at the work of other artists such as Henry Bone and Charles Muss.

Photographic Self-portrait

by Robert Cornelius, 1809–1893

Look at this man with his arms crossed staring right at us. This is the pioneering American photographer Robert Cornelius and he isn't staring at us but at his camera. He is taking the first ever self-portrait photograph in 1839 and he needs to stand motionless for about ten minutes or the photo will be blurred. Look at him trying not to fidget and the curiosity on his face. Any minute now, he will cover the lens to stop the exposure and then take his camera to a darkened room. There he will open it and take out the polished metal photographic plate inside. After bathing the plate in various chemicals, an image will 'develop' and Cornelius will see this image - the first ever selfie!

Who was he?
Robert Cornelius was born in Philadelphia, USA. He pioneered techniques that made early photography quicker and simpler.

This early sort of photograph was called a daguerreotype. It didn't use negative film like later cameras, but made an image directly onto a polished sheet of silver-plated copper.

 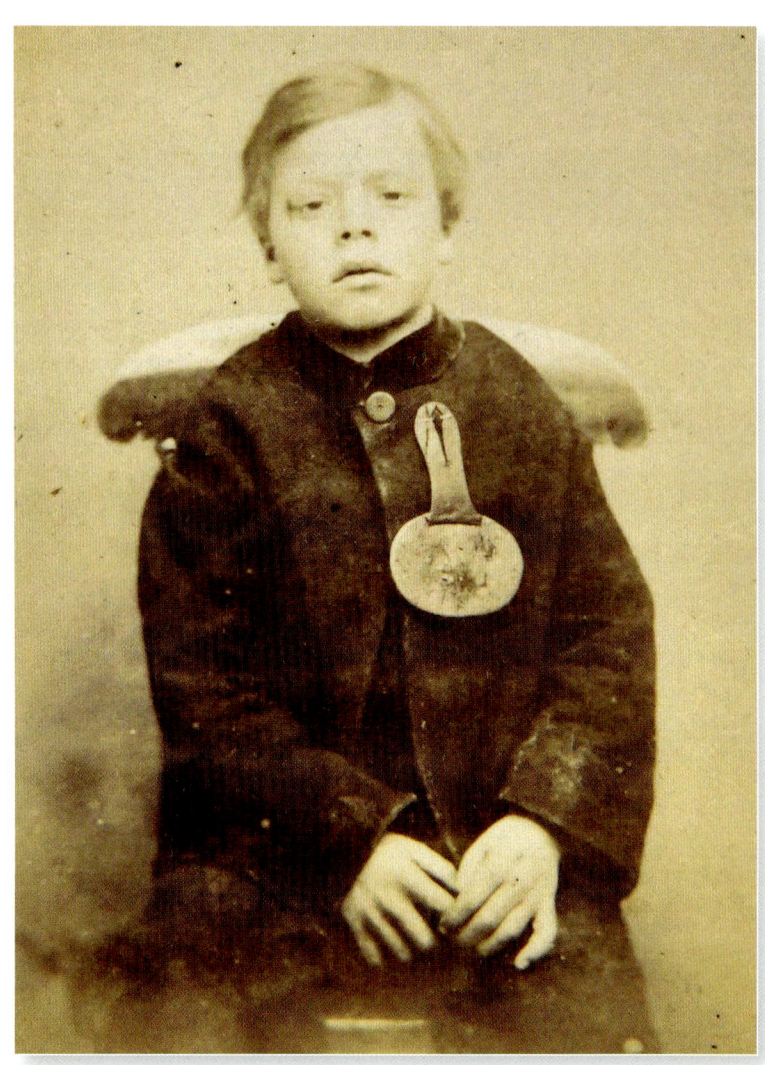

Child Criminals

by an unknown photographer

As early as the 1840s in England, the police began to take photographs that recorded the faces of the people they arrested. Such portraits became known as 'mugshots' and it revolutionised the identification of criminals. These three frightened children, photographed between 1873–1876, were unlucky enough to live in the days when the very young could be sent to adult prisons for committing the smallest of crimes. For example, the 11-year-old lad on the right was found guilty of stealing some cocoa powder, the 12-year-old girl, a warm cloak and the 10-year-old boy, 'items to the value of 8 pence'... It brings to mind Charles Dickens' 1830s novel, *Oliver Twist*, a story that urged society to protect children from poverty and exploitation rather than punish them for it.

Young children like this were locked up alongside hardened criminals.

I just wanted to know what cocoa tasted like, Sir ...

Berthe married Eugene Manet, the brother of another Impressionist, Eduard Manet. Their daughter, Julie, became a favourite model for portraits.

When Berthe Morisot was a student, France didn't allow women to attend art schools and she had to be taught privately.

Après le Déjeuner

by Berthe Morisot, 1841–1895

Unlike the noisy music hall paintings of other Impressionists such as Édouard Manet and Edgar Degas, Bertha Morisot captured quieter moments such as this gentle portrait from 1881. The title translates as 'after lunch' and we see a girl sitting in flickering light surrounded by flowers. The green grapes look delicious. Morisot used a 'wet on wet' technique of painting rather than waiting for each layer of slow-drying oil paint to dry. It allowed her and her fellow Impressionists to paint directly from life and capture changing light and colour.

Some people thought the Impressionist style 'messy' and when she exhibited alongside other Impressionists in 1874, one famous critic wrote that they were lunatics, adding '... of which one is a woman!'

Who was she?
The red-haired lady in the painting is Marie Renard, a professional model, who often posed for Berthe Morisot's paintings.

Berthe kept a notebook and wrote down her thoughts about the sexism she suffered as a female artist.

I don't think there has ever been a man who treated a woman as an equal ... I know that I am worth as much as them.

The Artist's Wife at a Sewing Table

by Vilhelm Hammershøi, 1864–1916

This portrait of the artist's wife Ida is typical of the painting style of Vilhelm Hammershøi. Completed in Denmark around 1897, It has such a peaceful atmosphere that you can almost imagine the tick-tock of a grandfather clock. He has painted it in muted tones letting the polished table reflect light onto Ida's face. Look at her strong hand, tightly holding the fabric, and the concentration on her face as she makes neat, tiny stitches. This is just one of many interior portraits painted by Hammershøi, many featuring his wife. Although some people may find his grey colour palette gloomy, his paintings reflect the style of Danish interior decor at the time and record those small everyday moments in life that so often go unnoticed.

Who was she?
Ida Ilsted was born in 1869 and she was the sister of an art student friend of Vilhelm's. They married in 1891. Although all seems peaceful in this portrait, Ida was reputed to have a fiery temper!

I'm going to paint you sewing, Ida!

What are you painting?

43

Portrait of Adele Bloch-Bauer

by Gustav Klimt, 1862–1918

Gustav Klimt was a founding member of an art group known as the Vienna Secession and this chic portrait of the wealthy Adele Bloch-Bauer from 1903 is a prime example of Klimt's work. He made many life studies of Adele but when it came to make the painting, he drew inspiration from a visit to Italy where he had seen Byzantine religious icons. Klimt's portrait is covered with gold leaf and uses gesso (a paint thickened with chalk) to create swirling patterns, geometric shapes and eye symbols inspired by ancient Egyptian art. It is Klimt's decorative masterwork and, as our eyes travel around the dream-like painting, it's hard to tell where Adele's fabulous dress ends and the background begins.

Who was she?
Adele and her husband Ferdinand Bloch-Bauer were wealthy art collectors. After her death, Ferdinand moved to Switzerland to escape Nazi persecution for being Jewish. This portrait was stolen by the Nazis and was only returned to the family in 2006.

The Byzantine era was a period of Roman rule over parts of eastern Europe from 330–1453. Have a look at some golden Byzantine icons.

I will make her as beautiful as a Byzantine icon.

Emil and Ada Nolde

by Emil Nolde, 1867–1956

What do you think of this self-portrait by the German painter Emil Nolde with his wife Ada, created in 1916? Look at him posing in his traditional, German folk costume staring at us with pale blue eyes. The wild brushstrokes, the clashing colours, the green shadows on his face and Ada's red-hot dress make a perfect example of the art movement Expressionism. However, despite his progressive views about modern art, Nolde had a dark side … he was a fanatical Nazi. He continued to support them even when his paintings were confiscated and mocked alongside other Expressionists as 'unGerman' at the Nazi-organised exhibition, 'Degenerate Art', in Munich in 1937. Throughout the Second World War (1939–1945), Nolde supported the Nazi's racist ideology and even reported fellow artists to Hitler's secret police. What do you think of the portrait now?

Nolde always claimed he had abandoned his Nazi beliefs long before the war but in 2013 historians discovered letters and documents that confirmed his Nazi support right until Hitler's defeat in 1945.

Who were they?
Hans Emil Hansen grew up on a farm near a village called Nolde. As a painter he associated with Expressionist artists and spent a lot of time in Berlin, where he met his Danish wife Ada Vilstrup who was a cabaret singer and dancer. They married in 1902 and that's when he changed his name to Nolde.

Look at the work of other Expressionist artists such as Edvard Munch and Franz Marc.

The Actor Ichikawa Sadanji II

by Natori Shunsen, 1886–1960

Natori Shunsen began his career as a newspaper illustrator in Tokyo, Japan, and went on to become a master printmaker of a Japanese art style known as Yakusha-e. These 'actor pictures' publicised the stars of the popular Japanese kabuki, a traditional form of Japanese theatre that mixes drama, music and dance with highly stylised costumes and masks. This portrait of the actor Ichikawa Sadanji II was made in 1926 using the ancient printmaking technique of woodblock. It was a perfect way to print multiple copies for the kabuki superstars' fans. Here we see Ichikawa striking a pose in his elaborate 'kumadori' stage makeup to play the wicked priest Narukami.

Who was he?
The actor Ichikawa Sadanji II (1880–1940) was Japan's most popular kabuki actor during the early 20th century.

The woodblock technique is similar in process to lino cutting. The parts that are not to be printed are carved away and colours are built up in layers.

The paper is pressed down on top and then peeled back to reveal the printed image.

49

Gamin

Augusta Savage, 1892–1962

The front of this sculpture is inscribed 'Gamin', a word once used to describe the urchins or 'streetwise' children of New York, USA. It's typical of the work of Augusta Savage who celebrated the people of poor areas of New York City, such as Harlem. Augusta was part of a revival of African-American culture, involving dance, art and fashion known as the Harlem Renaissance. As she struggled to become a successful artist, Augusta worked in a laundry as a day job to pay her bills.

In 1934 she became the first African-American artist to be elected to the National Association of Women Painters and Sculptors. She established her own teaching studio, The Savage Studio of Arts and Crafts, and co-founded the Harlem Artists' Guild, an organisation that helped African-American artists find employment.

Who was he?
This young man's name was Ellis Ford and he was Augusta's nephew who was visiting her in Harlem.

Why don't you make a sculpture of me, aunty?

American Gothic

by Grant Wood. 1891–1942

The story behind this well-known double-portrait painted by Grant Wood in 1930 began with a wooden house in Iowa, USA, that caught his artist's eye. It's built in a style known as Carpenter Gothic, and Wood felt inspired to paint who he imagined may have once lived there. To do this he asked his dentist and his sister to pose for him dressed up as settlers. His sister wears an old-fashioned print apron and the dentist grips a pitchfork – can you see that fork shape echoed in both the stitching of his overalls and shirt? In this portrait, Wood seems to be mimicking the style of an old-fashioned photograph from the days when people had to keep still for long periods of time (see Robert Cornelius, page 36). Perhaps that's why he has given them such serious expressions.

Who were they?
Nan Wood Graham and Dr Byron McKeeby are dressed as 19th century settlers. Wood himself grew up on a farm in rural Iowa and became part of the Regionalist art movement, a group of artists who chose to paint realistic scenes of small-town America.

Wood's paintings were influenced by the portraits and tronies of Dutch masters such as Vermeer and Van Eyck. When some people accused Wood of mocking Iowa farmers he denied this.

All the good ideas I've ever had came to me while I was milking a cow.

Coal Miner's Bath, Chester-le-street, Durham

by Bill Brandt, 1904–1983

This double-portrait by the photo-journalist Bill Brandt is very personal. It invites us into the kitchen of a coal miner to watch his wife scrubbing the coal-grime from his skin. Notice that wound on his back. Do you think he may have got this when crawling along the narrow underground passages of the coal mine? Notice his wife's polished shoes and the apron-dress she wears to keep her clothes clean. Can you see the soap on the mat and how she seems to be sharing a joke as she scrubs? Rather like the cool, quiet Hammershøi painting on page 42, this portrait captures a small everyday moment. But it's a very different moment to the quiet Danish interior – it's a coal miner's bath night and it's warm and splashy and there's laughter shared.

Who were they?
This couple lived in the north-east of England in the late 1930s at a period of great hardship called the Great Depression. Bill Brandt was a German-born British documentary photographer who had studied with the experimental artist-photographer Man Ray.

This was one of many photographs Brandt took of miners when he visited the north-east of England in 1937.

Put your head down or you'll get soap in your eyes.

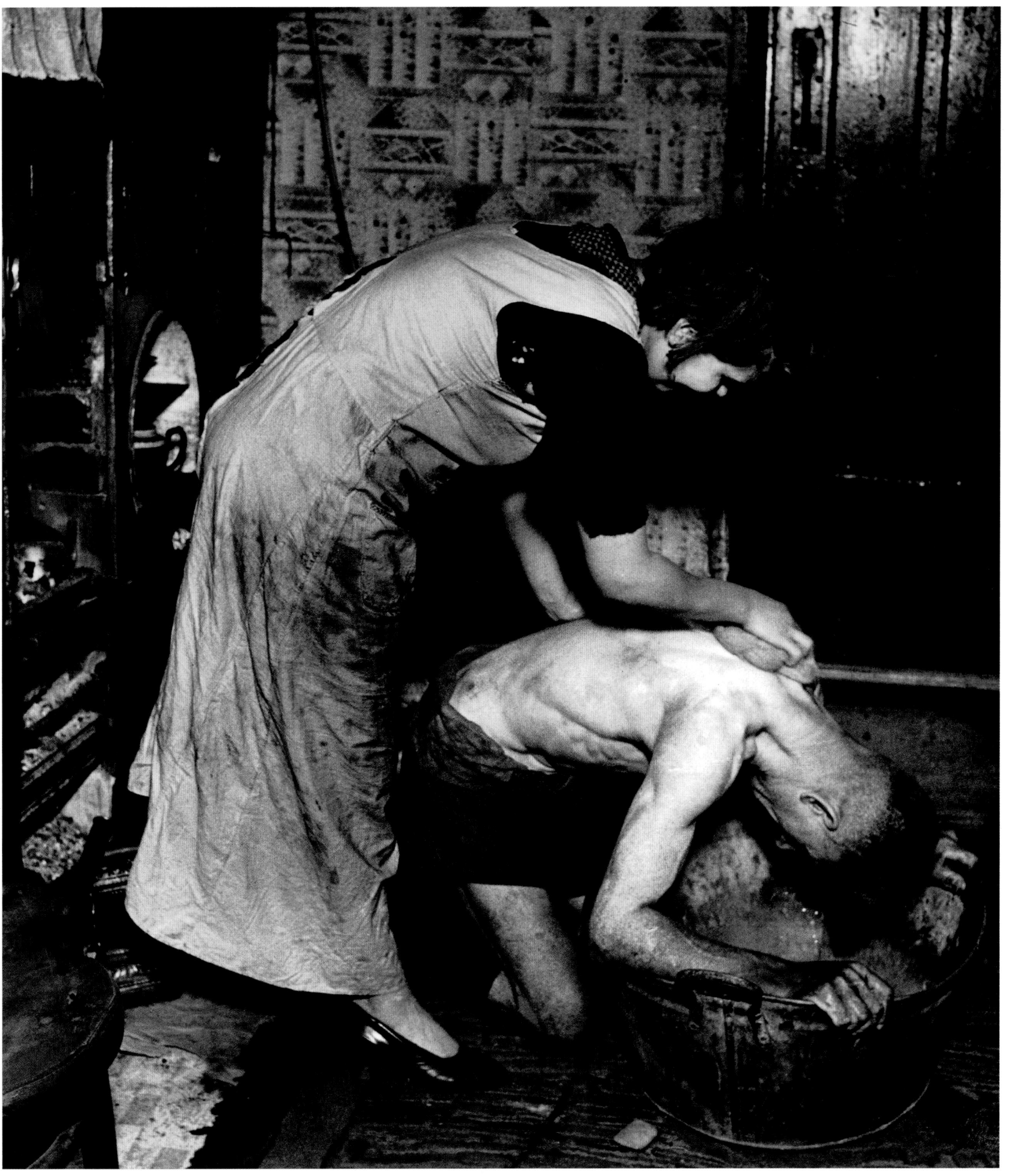

Thorn Necklace and Hummingbird

by Frida Kahlo, 1907–1954

The Mexican painter Frida Kahlo painted this self-portrait in 1940 just before she remarried her ex-husband, the famous painter and revolutionary Diego Rivera. She uses symbols from Mexican folk culture to show her mixed feelings about Rivera, who, after divorcing her only a few months earlier, now wanted to marry her again. That dead hummingbird around her neck is a Mexican love charm. Notice how its arched wings are echoed in Frida's eyebrows. That cat may be a symbol of bad luck, and that monkey may be Ozomatli, the companion of Xochipilli, the god of dance and music, as Frida and Diego famously loved music and dancing. But of course, the monkey also symbolises Diego Rivera. Look at him tightening a necklace of thorns around her neck.

Who was she?
At the age of 18 Frida Kahlo was terribly injured in a bus collision and underwent many operations. She began to paint in hospital to pass the time and, despite her injuries, became Mexico's most famous modern painter.

There have been two accidents in my life Diego ... and you are the worst.

Ruby Loftus Screwing a Breech-ring

by Dame Laura Knight, 1877–1970

This painting by the English artist Laura Knight was made during the Second World War in 1943. She was asked by the War Artists' Committee to paint a propaganda portrait of a highly-skilled female factory worker. At the time, the British government was finding it hard to recruit women for wartime factory work and Ruby Loftus, a skilled worker, was chosen for a recruitment drive. Knight's painting uses the spotlight to illuminate Ruby's look of concentration as she accurately shaves away the spiral of metal to make the screw thread of a breech-ring, while in the background other female workers are busy working hard. Laura and Ruby's story was featured in wartime newsreels and the painting became one of Laura Knight's most famous works.

Who was she?
Ruby was a 21-year-old worker at the Royal Ordnance Factory in Newport, Wales who had become an expert at the difficult task of cutting the breech-ring, an important part of an anti-aircraft gun.

Just hold that pose for me Ruby. What a noisy place this is!

I always loved to paint at the circus.

Dame Laura Knight was well-known for painting circus performers and ballet dancers before her wartime factory and RAF airbase commissions.

Self-portrait

by Gerard Sekoto, 1913–1993

This self-portrait is by a pioneer of black South African modern art, Gerard Sokoto. He painted this in 1947, the year he left his homeland for Paris. In France, as well as painting, he earned a living as a jazz musician. In Europe he came into contact with the work of modern art movements such as Impressionism and Expressionism. This confident self-portrait bathed in a greenish-yellow light and dramatic shadows shows the blend of the folk art he loved as well as the influence of Expressionist painters such as Emil Nolde (see page 46). Sekoto never forgot black South Africans' struggle against the racist political system known as apartheid. From France he painted the racism, the riots and the political turmoil of his home country, alongside peaceful remembered scenes of family life.

Sekoto was also a poet and a talented jazz musician, playing the piano in the clubs of Paris, France.

Who was he?
Gerard Sekoto grew up in a rural area of South Africa but then moved to Johannesburg and later Cape Town. Sekoto's paintings showing busy scenes of everyday life became successful. He was the first black artist to have a painting bought by a museum in South Africa. Yet, despite sell-out exhibitions he was so disgusted at the racism in his country that he moved to Paris.

Take your road and travel along ...

Seated Woman Drawn on a Chair

by Saul Steinberg, 1914–1999

Romanian-born Saul Steinberg was influenced by Dada and Surrealism and in this witty portrait, from 1950, we see elements of those art movements. Here we have a woman curled up in a chair with her hand on a table but when you look closely you see Steinberg has painted her directly onto the furniture. It's a clever visual trick that relies on the chair and table being photographed in the right position so that the painting of her arm lines up with the painting of her on the chair.

Steinberg named these images 'photoworks' and they include people sitting on furniture and even lying in bathtubs. Steinberg's witty style crossed art boundaries between illustration, caricature, painting, design and photography.

I don't quite belong to the art, cartoon or magazine world ... The art world doesn't quite know where to place me.

Guerrillero Heroico

by Alberto Korda, 1928–2001

This portrait of Che Guevara, by Alberto Korda, was taken in 1960 just after the Cuban revolution. Korda supported the revolution and, as we look up at his hero, Korda's composition may remind us a little of another revolutionary portrait, the one of Napoleon by Jacques-Louis David on page 32. As Che stares above our heads, notice how Korda allows the shadows of Che's long hair to slim his face and tighten his jaw, the same flattering trick used by Petrus Christus on page 14. To this day, for many people, this iconic image still symbolises the idea of rebellion. Many artistic interpretations of Che's face on posters and T-shirts have popularised Korda's original image still further.

Alberto Korda

Who was he?
Che Guevara (1928–1967) was born in Argentina with Spanish and Irish ancestors. He was well-educated and a trained doctor who became the second-in-command during Fidel Castro's Cuban revolution.

The Irish artist Jim Fitzpatrick (b. 1944) once met Che and years later made what would become a world-famous poster of Korda's image. He called it 'Viva Che!'.

I literally wanted it to breed like rabbits. I wanted it to spread!

65

Stylised Portrait of Jacqueline

by Pablo Picasso, 1881–1973

Pablo Picasso often used his wife Jacqueline Roque as a model for his experimental portraits. This one from 1962 is an example of Cubism, a type of abstract art that uses geometric shapes to present different views of the same subject from all angles. For example, in this graphic linocut what do you see first? Do you see Jacqueline looking straight at you or two faces in profile staring at one another? Are the profiles both Jacqueline or could it be the faces of Jacqueline and Picasso eye to eye? Look how Picasso has carefully considered the shapes he cut away, so allowing the white paper to make face shapes as well as the inked orange, yellow and black printings.

Who was she?
Jacqueline Roque was working at her cousin's pottery studio when she first met Picasso. They married in 1961. She was his second wife and he made over 400 portraits of her.

Jacqueline!

pour Armera fils
Picasso

67

Shot Sage Blue Marilyn

by Andy Warhol, 1928–1987

The American artist Andy Warhol was part of the Pop Art movement that began in the 1950s. It drew inspiration from everyday popular culture such as comic art, advertising art, films, TV shows and pop groups ... Warhol was fascinated by celebrities and his silkscreen portraits of the legendary film star Marilyn Monroe began in 1962, shortly after her death. For many, Marilyn represented the glamour of the 1950s and Warhol's portraits of her continued over many years, changing the colour of her make-up, hair and face and even making multiple Marilyn images to reflect her fame. This image is from 1964.

Warhol went on to make silkscreen portraits of many other celebrities but his portraits of Marilyn are now considered to be his masterpieces.

Who was she?
Norma Jeane Mortenson (1926–1962) changed her name to Marilyn Monroe. She became the most glamorous actress of her day. But off-camera Monroe's glamour led to her being pestered by both newspaper reporters and her fans. It led to an unhappy personal life.

Just look at you, gorgeous Marilyn!

To make his artwork, Andy Warhol often used silkscreen printing; a technique where a picture is printed one colour after another, by pressing inks through the stencil shapes in a mesh screen.

Buzz Aldrin on the Moon

by Neil Armstrong. 1930–2012

In 1969, Neil Armstrong was the first human to walk on the Moon and he took this portrait of his colleague Buzz Aldrin to prove it. Armstrong's clever composition has made sure the Moon's horizon passes exactly behind Buzz's eyes. Just like in da Vinci's *Mona Lisa* (page 18), this artists' 'trick' attracts our attention to Aldrin's head. That's when we realise Armstrong has also taken a self-portrait. There he is, reflected in Aldrin's mirror-like helmet. As he stands below the blue dot that is our far-away planet Earth, and with the lonely moonscape stretching away on all sides, Armstrong is proclaiming to the world that moonwalks are no longer science fiction but a scientific fact.

That's one small step for man, one giant leap for mankind.

Who were they?
They were US astronauts who walked on the Moon as part of the 1969 Apollo 11 mission. The third member of the team, Michael Collins, remained in lunar orbit with the command module Columbia.

As well as taking photographs, Armstrong made a live broadcast to Earth from the surface of the Moon.

David Bowie

by Masayoshi Sukita, 1938–

This iconic portrait by Masayoshi Sukita was one of a series of publicity shots taken for the musician David Bowie's 1973 concert tour of Japan. It was at a time when Bowie's theatrical, rock star stage persona, Ziggy Stardust had already taken the world by storm. Look at Bowie's fabulous kabuki-inspired costume designed by Kansai Yamamoto, and look at his stunning kabuki-style makeup by Yacco Takahashi ... Now check out the portrait of Ichikawa Sadanji II by Natori Shunsen on page 48. Bowie was fascinated by Japanese culture and loved kabuki and in this portrait both he and Sukita seem to be paying homage to that traditional Japanese art form.

By creating his own 'actor picture', Bowie was promising his fans that his up-coming 1973 tour would combine music, dance and fabulous costumes in a kabuki-style rock concert – and it did just that.

That's just the image I want for my Japanese tour!

We have turned you into a Yakusha-e.

My Dream of a Person with Birds

by Jessie Oonark, 1906–1985

After the dark days of winter, the return of nesting birds is a symbol of spring in many cultures. But there's more to this 1981 image by Jessie Oonark. After living a nomadic Arctic life for 50 years, one terrible winter a starving Jessie and her children had to be airlifted to the Inuit community at Baker Lake (also known as Qamani'tuaq). It was there that she began to make drawings. Jessie's father had been an Inuit shaman, one of the folk healers who believe they can use animal helpers to visit the spirit world. This print, made with linocut and stencil, is thought to be a portrait of a shaman. Look at the upward stare as he waits for take-off and the birds eagerly lining up on an arm and leg to whisk him away.

My Dream of a Person with Birds   6/50 1981 JESSIE OONARK/M. UKANTKU

Who were they?
The image shows someone who can communicate with nature and the spirit world. Jessie's unique prints were inspired by Inuit folk stories and magical beliefs. Her images were created in collaboration with skilled Inuit printmakers, in this case the artist Magdalene Ukpatiku (1931-1999).

Living conditions could be tough for nomadic Inuit families.

Magdalene helped me make my prints.

Untitled

by Cindy Sherman, 1954–

Cindy Sherman's work is about identity, examining a world dominated by celebrities in magazines, films and on social media. From her earliest works, such as a series of photographic portraits called *Untitled Film Stills*, Sherman has dressed herself up as: actresses, jilted girlfriends, unhappy housewives, high society ladies ... She has questioned female roles and even posed as characters from Classical paintings. Cindy Sherman's works re-invent the 'tronie', a style that you can read more about in *Girl with a Pearl Earring* by Vermeer on page 27. In this image from 1982, Cindy Sherman dresses up as actress Marilyn Monroe and she is inviting the viewer to examine the idea of 'glamour' just as Andy Warhol did, in his own way, on page 68.

Who was she?
Cindy Sherman often explores the idea of 'beauty' and this portrait of her as Marilyn Monroe (1926–1962) is a good example. Monroe was considered the most beautiful actress of her day but she soon became objectified as fans became so obsessed with her glamorous image they forgot about the lonely real-life person behind the makeup.

I wish I could treat every day as Halloween, and get dressed up and go out into the world as some eccentric character.

© Cindy Sherman.Chromographic Color print. 20 x 16 inches. Courtesy the artist and Hauser & Wirth:76."l.

The Policeman's Daughter

by Paula Rego. 1935–2022

Paula Rego's paintings and pastel drawings focus on human rights, particularly women's rights, and are often influenced in style by the folk tales told to her by her grandmother and the work of artists such as Goya. They can be dreamlike and sometimes nightmarish but they always tell stories. Black leather jackboots are a world-wide symbol of dictatorships and secret police and in this 1987 portrait we see a grim-faced and obediant young woman polishing her father's jackboot to a mirror-like shine. It's unsettling, and all the more so for not showing the father. Yet, perhaps he is there ... look at that cat. Doesn't it seem to be standing on jackboot-shaped back legs with its paw in a fascist salute?

Who was she?

The daughter in the painting was modelled on drawings Paula made of her own daughter. Paula was born in Portugal, but later moved to the UK. When she was born, Portugal was ruled under a dictatorship known as the Estado Novo (1933–1974). Many viewers see the daughter as a symbol of the lack of freedoms some women experienced in Portugal at this time.

Is this a good pose, mum?

Don't just cuddle the boot – give it a good polish!

Little Amal

Handspring Puppet Company. 2021

With her name meaning 'hope' in Arabic, Little Amal represents a 10-year-old refugee travelling across Europe in search of her mother. Built by a team of designers and artists from the Handspring Puppet Company of South Africa, she became the star attraction of The Walk, a travelling art festival. Journeying from the Syrian-Turkish border, Little Amal walked tall through 65 towns across Turkey, Greece, Italy, France, Switzerland, Germany, Belgium and the UK. Little Amal drew attention to the plight of refugees and she provoked strong emotional responses wherever she went – from being loved and cheered by well-wishing crowds to enduring stone-throwing and racist abuse. In 2023 Little Amal completed a 6,000-mile (9,656-km) journey across the USA.

Who is she?
Little Amal represents refugees everywhere. She came from a collaboration between The Walk Productions, a not-for-profit company, and Good Chance, a theatre group formed after a visit to a refugee camp in Calais, France. Three puppeteers operate Little Amal, including one inside to control her head, eyes and mouth..

Hold her steady!

We can make her come to life by moving her hands.

Little Amal's message is clear: 'Don't forget us – we're just like you'd be if you lost your home and family.'

Self-portrait with Dingo

by Vincent Namatjira, 1983–

This satirical self-portrait by the indigenous Australian artist Vincent Namatjira was painted in 2022 when Queen Elizabeth II of the UK was still alive. Vincent has cheekily painted himself slouched in her throne holding a paintbrush and propping his dusty boots on a bucket of paint. Instead of the Queen's pampered corgis, Vincent has chosen a wild Australian dingo dog as a symbol of his own ancestral origins. Perhaps Vincent is gently questioning if Australia should remain loyal to the far-away British monarchy or become a republic – or perhaps he is making the point that all people should be equal.

Vincent's work focuses on power, wealth, politics and history and often features famous faces, from the British royal family to historical figures such as Captain Cook. Vincent's witty, bold and expressive paintings make us smile but also make us think and ask questions.

Who is he?
Vincent was born in the Northern Territory but after his mother died he was placed in foster care. When he turned 18 Vincent re-connected with his roots, language and culture. He is now one of Australia's most talented modern painters.

When I paint the Queen or the King ... it's like taking away their power, putting us level with the rest of the world.

Vincent's great-grandfather, Albert Namatjira, was a famous landscape artist who once shook hands with Queen Elizabeth II.

Glossary

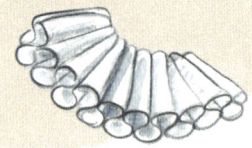

Abstract (art): art that uses colours and shapes for visual effect.

Apartheid: A policy of separating people because of their race or colour.

Byzantine: The name given to the empire centred in Byzantium (modern Istanbul) that controlled land around the Mediterranean from the 4th to 15th centuries. Sometimes called the Eastern Roman Empire.

canvas: A cloth stretched on a frame to paint on, usually made of linen or cotton.

caricature: A picture or cartoon that exaggerates a person's features to dramatic or humorous effect.

Carpenter Gothic: An American form of architecture using Gothic motifs such as turrets or arches.

Catholic: A form of Christianity.

chiaroscuro: The use of strong light and shadow in a painting.

Christian: A follower of, or relating to, the religion based on the teachings of Jesus Christ.

Classical art: A realistic style inspired by ancient Greek and Roman art.

colonial: A land and its people ruled by another country, for example, when Britain ruled India.

composition: The way a painting is planned or designed.

court: In relation to royalty, the place where the royal family live and the people who live with them, making it a centre of power.

Cuban revolution: An armed uprising led by Fidel Castro in Cuba, the Caribbean, in 1959.

Cubism: A revolutionary, early 20th-century painting style where images were built up using geometric shapes and sometimes collage.

Dada: An art movement that began in 1916 that poked fun at the modern world.

dictatorship: A government led by a dictator that rules with absolute power and without free elections.

Expressionism: An early 20th-century art movement originating in Germany where artists tried to paint their emotions and moods.

genre: A style of art.

Ice Age: A period of time between 70,000 to 10,000 years ago when about one-third of planet Earth was covered in ice.

Impressionism: An art movement originating in France in the 1860s where artists tried to capture the impressions of the moment, especially of light and colour.

Inuit: The native peoples of the Arctic regions.

jazz: A rhythmic and often wild style of music first popular in the 1920s.

Jewish: Describes the people who trace their roots back to the Hebrews of the Eastern Mediterranean who founded the religion of Judaism.

kabuki: The name for a special style of Japanese drama.

kumadori: Traditional Japanese face makeup using bold and colourful patterns used in kabuki.

Medieval: A long period of world history from 500 CE to 1500 CE.

merchant: Someone who makes a living by buying and selling goods.

model: Someone who poses for an artist to draw or paint.

mugshot: A photograph taken by the police of crimel suspects.

Napoleonic Wars: A series of battles fought between Napoleon Bonaparte's French Empire and a European alliance that included Britain and Germany.

Nazi: The far-right National Socialist Party led by Adolf Hitler that came to power in Germany from 1930 until their defeat by allied forces during the Second World War.

nomadic: People that don't live in one place and sometimes follow the seasonal migrating animals.

oil paint: A type of paint made from coloured powder mixed with oil.

Glossary

pioneering: Using new ideas and methods.

Pop Art: Art inspired by 'popular culture' such as magazines and TV shows.

portrait: A painting, drawing, sculpture or photograph of a person.

power-portrait: A portrait intended to make someone look powerful.

propaganda: Information used to promote a cause or political point of view.

publicity shot: Photograph taken to publicise someone and used in magazine or social media.

RAF: The Royal Air Force.

refugee: Someone who has left their own home or country to escape war or natural disasters.

religious icon: Used in some Christian traditions to portray holy figures such as Jesus or the Virgin Mary.

Renaissance: A time when European artists, writers and scientists began to think about the world in new ways at the same time as rediscovering the art and learning of the Romans and the Greeks. It lasted several centuries (13th to 16th) and happened at different times in different countries.

Romantic: Describes a painting style dominant in the early 19th century that looked to ancient myths and the natural world for its subject matter.

Royal Academy: The Royal Acadmey of Arts is an institution in London set up in the 18th century by artists to encourage and exhibit art.

satirical: Art that makes fun of or criticises someone, often used to make a political point.

sculptor: An artist who makes art in three dimensions, often by carving wood, metal or stone.

Second World War: The world war of 1939 to 1945. It was fought between Germany, Italy and Japan on the one side against Allied forces on the other that included Britain, Canada, Australia, New Zealand, India and the USA and many other countries. The Allied forces won.

self-portrait: A drawing, painting, sculpture or photograph of yourself.

Surrealism: A mid 20th-century movement in art and literature which explored the world of dreams and fantasy.

terracotta: A type of clay that is fired in a kiln to make pottery.

tronie: A type of portrait common in 17th century Dutch painting where an artist's model is dressed to symbolise something such as wealth or innocence or some kind of religious idea.

Vienna Secession: A decorative style of Austrian art begun in 1897 and related to Art Nouveau which is a style of art from the 1890s that included flowing lines and plant shapes.

Werewolf syndrome: Another name for Hypertrichosis, a rare condition when excessive hair grows all over the human body.

Index

For Melker Granström 1940 – 2023

Franklin Watts
First published 2025
Hodder & Stoughton Limited

Credits: *Editor:* Paul Rockett
Cover design: Peter Scoulding
Design: Peter Scoulding, based on an original
concept developed by Jonathan Hair and
Mick Manning.
Picture researcher: Diana Morris

Picture credits:

The Print Collector/Alamy: 4c; De Agostini/M.Seemüller/Gettty Images: 4bl; C.M.Dixon/Hertage Images/Getty Images: 5t; DnDavis/Shutterstock: 5c; Simone Crespiatico/Shutterstock: 5b; Ezra Collection/Alamy: 6.
Paul Markillie/Alamy: 7t; St Catherine's Monastery, Sinai/Wikimedia PD: 7b; Jaroslav Moravcik/Shutterstock: 8; Taipei Palace Museum, Taipei/Wikimedia PD: 11; Metropolitan Museum, NY/Wikimedia PD: 13; Gemalde Gallerie,Vienna/Google Arts & Culture/Wikimedia PD: 14.; Albertina Museum, Vienna/incamerastock/Alamy: 16; The Louvre, Paris/dcoetzee/Wikimedia PD 18; Peter Horree/Alamy:b cover c, 21; Private Collection/Bonhams London/Bridgeman Images: 22; El Prado, Madrid/fernando maquiera/Wikimedia PD: 24-25; Google Arts & Culture/Wikimedia PD: fr cover br, 26; Photopat/Alamy: 29; GL Archive/Alamy: 30-31.; Ian Dagnell Computing/Alamy: 33; Private Collection/Phillip Mould & Co: 34; GL Archive/Alamy: 37; Dorset History Centre: fr cover cl, 38-39; agefotostock/Alamy: 40–41; National Museum of Art, Architecture and Design, Norway/Wikimedia CCA 4.0 International: 42; Antiquarian Images/Alamy: 45; Emil Nolde, A & E Nolde, 1916, oil on canvas, 89 x 74 cm. © Nolde Stiftung Seebüll: 46; Penta Springs Limited/Alamy: fr cover bc, 49; Courtesy of the Cleveland Museum of Art: Gamin, c.1929. © Augusta Savage (American 1892-1962). Hand-painted plaster, overall: 44.5 x 24.2 x 20.4 cm (17 1/2 x 91/2 x 81.16 in). Purchase from the J.H.Wade Fund 2003.40: 50; Giorgio Morara/Alamy: fr cover, tl, 52; © Bill Brandt Archive Ltd: 55; Artchives/Alamy/Estate of Frida Kahlo: 56; Imperial War Museum, London/wikimedia commons/PD: 59; Self portrait by Gerard Sekoto, 1947 © Gerard Sekoto Foundation/DALRO, South Africa/DACS, London 2025: 61; Photogènes: Commission for Flair Magazine,1950: 62; Alberto Korda/CPA Media/Alamy: 64; Photo Album/Alamy. Stylised portrait of Jacqueline by Pablo Picasso, 1962. Private Collection. © Succession Picasso/DACS London 2025: 67; Photo Christie's Images/Bridgeman Images. Shot Sage Blue Marilyn Monroe by Andy Warhol 1964. Graphic Interpretation of an original Andy Warhol artwork created in 2025 by Hachette. Andy Warhol and Andy Warhol artwork © 2025 The Andy Warhol Foundation for Visual Arts, Inc./Licensed by DACS, London 2025. Used with permission: 69; Neil Armstrong/NASA: 70; Masayoshi Sukita: © The estate of the artist: 73; © The estate of Jesse Oonark, courtesy of The Public Trustee, Nunavut. Photo credit Heffel Fine Art Auction House: 74; © Cindy Sherman.Chromographic Color print. 20 x 16 inches. Courtesy the artist and Hauser & Wirth: 77; © Estate of Paula Rego. All rights reserved 2025/licenced via Bridgeman Images: 78; Mario Tama/Getty Images: 81; Photo Don Arnold/Getty Images/ Vincent Namatjira, Self Portrait with Dingo, 2022, Art Gallery NSW © Vincent Namatjira /Copyright Agency. Licensed by DACS, London 2025:83.

Quotes:

P. 39 Berthe Morisot's diary entry, 1890; P. 53 Grant Wood, originally published in an article in the *New York Herald Tribune*, 2 June, 1974; P. 60 Gerard Sekoto, quote taken from one of his letters; P. 63 Steinberg, 'Straight from the Hand and Mouth of Steinberg,' Jean Vanden Heuvel, *LIFE Magazine*, 10 December 10, 1965; P. 64 Jim Fitzpatrick, 1967. P. 70 Neil Armstrong, One Small Step, transcript of Apollo 11 Moon landing, 20 July, 1969; P. 76 Cindy Sherman, 'A Conversation with Cindy Sherman', John Waters, *The Museum of Modern Art*, New York, 2012; P. 82 Vincent Namatjira, 'On Colonialism Satire and his Great Grandfather's Legacy', *The Guardian*, 16 October 2023.

HB ISBN 978 1 4451 9075 4

Printed in China.

Franklin Watts
An imprint of Hachette Children's Group
Part of The Watts Publishing Group, Carmelite House
50 Victoria Embankment, London EC4Y 0DZ

An Hachette UK Company
www.hachette.co.uk
www.franklinwatts.co.uk

The authorised representative in the EEA is Hachette
Ireland, 8 Castlecourt Centre, Dublin 15, D15 XTP3,
Ireland (email: info@hbgi.ie)

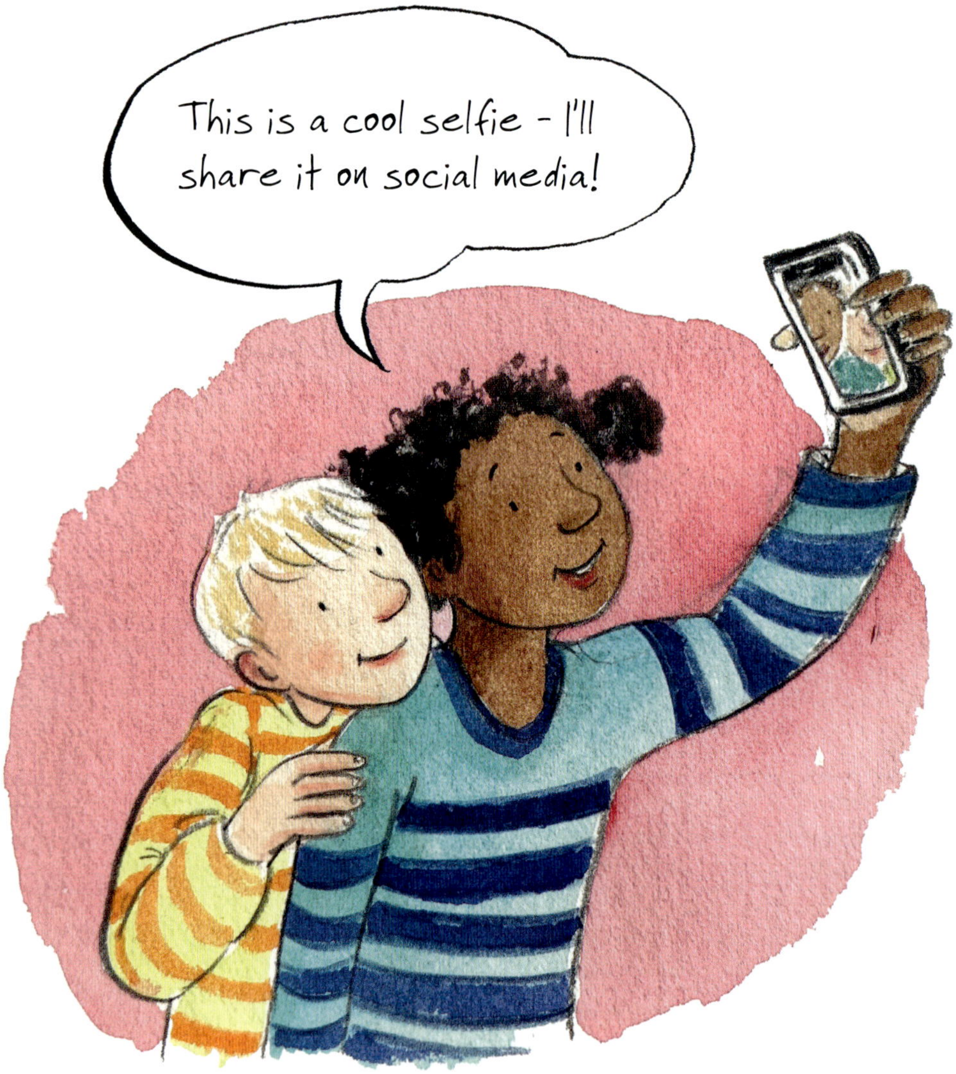
This is a cool selfie - I'll share it on social media!